Progressions of the Mind

Progressions
OF THE MIND

POEMS BY
David Berman

ABLE MUSE PRESS

Able Muse Press

www.ablemusepress.com

Library of Congress Cataloging-in-Publication Data

Names: Berman, David, 1934-2017, author.
Title: Progressions of the mind / poems by David Berman.
Description: San Jose, CA : Able Muse Press, 2021. | Summary: "Progressions of the mind is the posthumous and first full-length poetry collection by David Berman"-- Provided by publisher.
Identifiers: LCCN 2020000740 (print) | LCCN 2020000741 (ebook) | ISBN 9781773490618 (paperback) | ISBN 9781773490724 (digital)
Subjects: LCGFT: Poetry.
Classification: LCC PS3552.E724958 P76 2021 (print) | LCC PS3552.E724958 (ebook) | DDC 811/.54--dc23
LC record available at https://lccn.loc.gov/2020000740
LC ebook record available at https://lccn.loc.gov/2020000741

Printed in the United States of America

Cover image: *Mazed Mind* by Matze Bob

Cover & book design by Alexander Pepple

Able Muse Press is an imprint of *Able Muse: A Review of Poetry, Prose & Art*—at www.ablemuse.com

Able Muse Press
467 Saratoga Avenue #602
San Jose, CA 95129

Acknowledgments

On behalf of the author, Able Muse Press thanks the editors of the following journals where many of these poems originally appeared, sometimes in earlier versions:

Counter Measures: "The Prisoner," "Evidence of Being Human," "*De Senectute*," "Mother-in-Law," and "Unchanged"

Cumberland Poetry Review: "The Nonagenarian's Daughter's Complaint" and "The Now of Nature's Art"

Edge City Review: "Divorce Court" and "Rural Christmas"

Epigrammatist: "A Reproach to the Reproacher"

The Formalist: "No Doubt?," "Unrecited Declaration," "Why I Waited (I)," "Witches," "The Inexplicable," "A Song for Lazarus," "Bach," "Sacrifice," "Did You," "His Ex-Wife's Birthday," "The Cave Dweller," "Veiled Events," and "Mockingbird Call"

Iambs and Trochees: "The Poet's Drug," "Galatians," "Male, Female, and the Church Fathers," "For Mr. First," "Old Chairs," and "Early January"

Identity: "Unwritten Letter" and "Travelogue"

Light: "Reminders"

Piedmont Literary Review: "The Convergence of the Circus Animals"

Pivot: "A Soliloquy for Gabriel"

Poetry Digest: "Weekend Grandchildren"

The Powow River Poets Anthology II: "The Effect of Hearing the Sublime"

Sparrow: "Recalling What Would Have Been Aunt Mary's Ninety-Sixth Birthday," "Progressions of the Mind," "Settled," "Dutiful," "Sound and Light," "At Fifty-Nine," "To One Who Described His Religious Preference as 'Agnosticism,'" "Amos," "Ezekiel," and "The Plagiarists"

"Progressions of the Mind" appeared in *The Powow River Anthology*, Alfred Nicol, editor (Ocean Publishing, 2006).

"No Doubt?," "A Song for Lazarus," and "Veiled Events" appeared in *Sonnets: 150 Contemporary Sonnets*, William Baer, editor (University of Evansville Press, 2005).

Contents

Progressions of the Mind

Progressions of the Mind

1

"Our colored lady," as my mother called
Her part-time maid, would talk to me about
The Bible and her church. When summer stalled
Until it seemed sheer folly to go out
And face the Southern heat, I followed her
Around the house, absorbed at least a bit
Of what she had to say, though some things were
Beyond my understanding. One thing hit
Me plain, however: she believed that those
Who went to hell retained full memory
Of earthly life that would not decompose
And knew they were not where they wished to be,
While those in heaven could not recognize
Themselves or others seen with heavenly eyes.

2

Themselves or others seen with heavenly eyes
They knew as angels—is there not a verse
In Matthew that implies that marriage dies
When spouses do? She asked what could be worse
For bliss than watching through eternity
Your child or mama suffering in hell,
However justly earned that place might be,
And then she answered as if to dispel
All doubt, "The saints ain't gonna suffer there;
The Lord won't let that happen." Too young to
Dispute her logic, still I felt somewhere
Within, that what she said did not ring true
But lacked the words to ask, "How can one be
Immortal who forgets mortality?"

3

How can one be immortal who forgets
Mortality? I never quite forgot
What she had said; long after she had left—
Few maids outstayed a year and, like as not,
Deserted for the snowbirds in December—
I found out that her father and one son
Had both served time. For what, I don't remember.
She must have thought whatever they had done
Would keep them out of heaven. Back then, black
Churches leaned upon such women for
Existence; it made sense to say, "Alack,
The men who love and hurt you, who ignore
Your summons to repent—once you have died,
You will forget them on the other side."

4

You will forget them on the other side—
One who makes sociology out of
Religion will find both unjustified:
Not only the oppressed know that they love
Some who, if there is heaven, likely will
Be going elsewhere, all denial spent,
Nor are the persons hell-bound always male.
To love on earth is never to relent;
Love bears it out beyond the edge of doom.
Is heaven different? Could a mother bear
To hear her child gasp in another room,
Forever barred to her, and just not care?
If to be saved is to go on like this,
Hell's blight is no more harsh than heaven's bliss.

5

Hell's blight is no more harsh than heaven's bliss,
If those in heaven know of and are grieved
By the afflictions felt in the abyss
(Which may explain why Origen believed
That all, including Satan, at the end,
Would find salvation and why purgatory
Was first devised). But how can life extend
Beyond itself and yet not know the story
Of its own being? Disembodied souls
Assembled anywhere are hard enough
To comprehend for those whom flesh makes whole;
Without a brain and all the other stuff
That makes a body, and without a past,
A soul is but a sigh in a gale's blast.

6

A soul is but a sigh in a gale's blast,
Invisible and too ephemeral
To matter if indeed it does exist.
Who, contemplating the material
By which we live, has failed to think this thought?
And if a soul does nothing but return,
Inert, to God, this thought seems—does it not?—
Most likely true. Whereas, if souls that burn
In hell (if that's what souls there do) retain
Their human consciousness, one might elect
To go there and be stoic about pain.
Might or might not. The human intellect
Grasps less than it imagines, but mere rest
Is not fit contemplation for the blessed.

Is not fit contemplation for the blessed
To be with God and leave the rest to Him,
Above all, leave those questions unaddressed
No mind will ever answer? Minds grow dim;
I watched my mother's fade as mine will too;
She and the "colored ladies" are long dead.
Yet minds were made to sort out false from true
And, where the sorting is inhibited,
To speculate, and speculations lead
To unmapped worlds. My mother's voice I hear
Call out, "You're in her way. Go out and weed
The garden." "No, I'm not," I persevere.
"A boy should mind his mama," sadly drawls
Our colored lady as my mother calls.

A Song for Lazarus

My soul, where have you been these many days
My eyes were closed in dreamless sleep? I woke,
And all the sleepy town arose and spoke
Of wonder till the air was set ablaze
With flaming talk. And change. The skeptic prays
While the devout repeatedly invoke
Odd precedents. The ordinary folk
Would like to ask—I see it in their gaze—
What happened, but they fear to learn and so
Walk past me blindly. Not that there is much
To tell, and what there is, is negative:
No trumpet sounded, no lights came aglow.
My soul returned, and I, unfit to touch,
Decayed, stood up, because my Friend said: Live.

Heaven

I try imagining it. I cannot.
First, living in a place where time has no
Significance appears preposterous.
Besides, the ones who dwell there neither lust
Nor eat and drink and, thus, must do without
The satisfactions gained from sex and food.
But do they speculate? Why would they when
All answers to all questions lie at hand?

Jonathan Edwards had them witnessing
The torments of the damned—his heaven, so
To speak, an outsized Colosseum where
The prey deserved the lion's maulings and
The spectators had nothing else to do
But watch and watch and watch and watch and watch.

Veiled Events

You did not think about it long. Why should
You have? The slip (two numerals transposed)
You blamed on being harried. When you closed
The window on your hand, the likelihood
That this was one of more odd things you would
Be doing seemed remote. And when you dozed
Off at the theatre, you, of course, supposed
It due to nothing, nothing that a good
Night's sleep would not relieve. It's only now
That missed connections, unremembered names
Define too large a part of living to
Ignore that veiled events begin to show
You what they meant: the dread beyond all blames,
The furtive darkness closing in on you.

Witches

They are not gone.
They dwell within;
they sour your milk,
inflame your skin,

estrange your wife,
excite your cat,
exhume your dead—
they're good at that.

The bell is broken;
the candle, burned;
the book is missing—
untaught, unlearned,

such doubtful arts—
besides, you doubt
such remedies
can force them out.

And they predict
as in *Macbeth*
(because you let
them), life and death.

To One Who Described His Religious Preference as "Agnosticism"

Intellectually, I suspect,
We are agnostics all, but faith does not
Lie in the bosom of the intellect,
Where age and cares corrupt and treasures rot.
"But I cannot behold him," Job cried out;
"No man hath seen God," John, the most renowned
Of saints, declared. Though telescopes may scout
Infinity, no lens has yet been ground
To bring God into focus; I suspect
None ever will be, but who knows, who knows?
Intellectually, I reject
Cosmologies with God at head or toes,
But faith, that *fine invention*, sees where light
Illumines nothing but eternal night.

Unrecited Declarations

We hold these truths
until they drop
or we or both
do. Then we shop

for truths a bit
more portable,
more up-to-date.
Our hands too full

already and
not really strong,
the stern demands
of truths held long

add to their weight,
make them seem rough,
still good, but not
quite good enough.

Sacrifice

It means: I give up something that is mine
For God, for you, for others who
May give up something too
For many more—not something that they would
Have got along without just fine,
But something they thought good
Enough to fight to keep. Strange, looking back,
To say that though I gave, I never
Sacrificed. However
Generous my gift appeared, I gave
Only that which seemed to lack
A rationale to save,

Nothing with which I could not bear to part,
Nothing that came quivering from the heart.

The Now of Nature's Art

I drive into a sea of gold;
The trees with their November leaves
Bathed in a cloudy, faint, and cold
November sunset shine like sheaves
Of gold suspended from the sky,
And buildings that would otherwise
Be nondescript now glorify
Themselves by wearing gold disguise.
I know such grace as this must lapse,
Accept ephemerality
As given, welcome it perhaps;
It is not good for eyes to be
Focused too long on sights as rare
As more grace than the heart can bear.

Unwritten Letter

A hundred times I've written you this letter
And just as often changed it so that now
I can't recall the first one anyhow
Or even say I like the new one better.

You need not take back words you never uttered;
So went the smug cliché you used to quote.
Now stubborn words are sticking in my throat
Where they were formed but never even muttered.

For you, the unreturning argonaut,
I keep a journal in my mind and make
You make your comments on a sheet of thought.

Within that mind your voice stays strangely fresh;
Yet, though you've grown so much a listener
I could no longer bear the man you were,
I yearn for one more glimpse of you as flesh.

Divorce Court

It was a bright September day—or was
It June?—when they rushed down the aisle to sounds
Of Mendelssohn—or was it?—now it does
Not matter, not one whit. They both have grounds;
They did already that bright Saturday.
He'd been unfaithful as a lover, and
She knew it; she had been a fiancée
Who thought her slightest wish was his command,
And as she thought, she acted. Now, six years,
Two children later, they will face a judge
Who will pronounce them man and wife no more
And yet not strangers. Each one bears a grudge
For wasted time, for not saying before
That Saturday, "Is this not a mistake?"
For a coarse rift instead of a clean break.

The Inexplicable

Donna's wake: her best friend, Shirley, said,
"You know that Charlie killed her." I replied,
"You should have damn good proof before you spread
such rumors." So I kept my thoughts inside.

But Charlie knew machinery like no
one else I ever knew; he saw things whole
and fast. An accident such as the blow-
up of a stove?—he would know each control
on any stove he touched. And, yes, he was
as crooked as an old Palermo lane,
and one who craves dishonest dollars does
not scruple much. But what I can't explain
is Shirley, who, not fearing for her life,
took Donna's place as Charlie's part-time wife.

Why I Waited

1

I knew he killed her, knew it when I heard
he had been in the car with her when she
was killed. For though I never said a word
till he was safely dead, he had asked me—
and we were barely friends—to do the job.
(How many more must he have also tried!)
I told him to get someone from the Mob,
and he said he was joking. That he lied
was pretty clear. Now, my wife asks me why
I kept my mouth shut even after they
accused some black guy. How can I reply?
For if I answered, I would have to say
more than a guy like me would tell his wife
about the dark recesses of his life.

2

Was I afraid? That would be an excuse,
for even in a town where guys talked tough,
he and his gang were terrors on the loose,
who back in middle school pulled off some stuff
whose brazenness had hard ex-cons amazed.
On many an up-and-coming punk they left
a bloody face, an ego badly fazed,
a reputation hopelessly bereft
of clout. But fear of him was not what kept
me back. It didn't even cross my mind.
His gang was gone, and he himself now stepped
out with the swells. He likely wouldn't find
out I had talked. Fear is a reason I
can give my wife, a useful alibi.

3

In high school, tired of virginity
and shower stories made up after gym,
I forced a girl, and terrified that she
would tell the cops, I went and hired him
to keep her quiet. I stole sixty bucks
to pay him, and the story went away.
(Yeah, yeah, I know it might have been dumb luck.)
I felt a little grateful—should I say?—
and I would guess that's why he came to me.
But gratitude, like leather soles, wears thin.
Besides, this was a business deal; his fee
was huge for those days. So I can't begin
to call my silence a repayment, but
I understood just how the cards were cut.

4

Two years of college, then my girl forgot
to take her pill—at least that's what she said.
She would not touch abortion; so I got
a mover's job. I do not wish her dead—
don't get me wrong—but if our kids were grown
and she was gone, I would find someone new.
Eleven married years I have not known
the sex or love I once expected to.
But if I can't say whom I love, I know
exactly what I hate: the clock that wakes
me up each morning, and the boring, slow
day that ensues. I understand what makes
a guy think half a million bucks is worth
stashing a wife forever in the earth.

5

I could have called her—maybe others did—
I would have used a pay phone, let her know
her husband was attempting to get rid
of her. Would she have bought? Or just thought, *Oh
someone's making trouble?* I had heard—
or did I just concoct this story when
I knew the end of hers?—fights had occurred
in which her face was pummeled, but she then
told people she had walked into a wall
or been hit by a door. And what about
all the insurance he insisted on?
Would such a call have raised the final doubt?
Or was her understanding so far gone
it would have done no good? His dick was big.
Was that what kept her married to a pig?

6

His suicide: spectacular, a dive
a hundred feet into a river. Did
he really think had he remained alive,
they would have nailed him? Wonder if he hid
the loot, who has it now. The cops must have
known more than they let on. I got the news
while moving a piano for a suave
old gentleman who plainly loved his booze.
He'd offered me a drink, and I said *No.*
(Company regulations were quite clear.)
But after finding out, I craved one so
intensely that I asked him for a beer.
He must have read a strangeness in my face;
asked, "Did you know him?" I stared into space.

7

That night I told my wife, who lectured me.
I yelled, "Well, would you rather have me dead?"
And then I told the cops, who seemed to see
a public finally less interested.
The press was slamming them for false arrest
of that black dude. They said they would review
the info and get back. As I had guessed,
he had asked others, who had waited too
and then come forward. No book offers came
although I tried, and no paid interviews.
The reason why I waited was the same
As why he killed her: I had hoped to use
his "joke" to garner interest—big, tax-free—
on that old sixty bucks he got from me.

His Ex-Wife's Birthday

It's nothing he's supposed to celebrate;
Yet when that day arrives, it brings
Perverse rememberings
Connected with it: presents tied with strings
Instead of ribbons, bought so late
There wasn't time to wait

While they were being wrapped the way they should
Have been; her mock (but was it mock?)
Offense that drew his stock
And just as mock contrition; then the clock,
Warning them that soon they would
Miss dinner at the good

French bistro they both liked. How can he mend
This hole in life he cannot comprehend?

To You, Anonymously

My fingers touched the dial pad but did not
Quite make the call. Without a thing to say,
I would have done it had I known a way
To give it purpose, make it seem a lot
Less obvious that neediness had brought
Me to the point of being game to play
The games I had detested in my day
When they were played on me and I would plot
The quickest route to getting rid of bores
Without a total crash. You did not hear
From me last night; I thought it better to
Assuage my pride and hide my running sores
Than hazard letting my sad state appear
Even to one compassionate as you.

Weekend Grandchildren

They are polite but curious about
Things we would least suspect: that some clocks chime
And others don't, why teapots have straight spouts
And coffee pots' are crooked. We make time
For them, who seem to us to have abundant
Time, whilst they are patient with our gait,
Refrain from showing us that we're redundant
(Who neither teach nor parent), violate
No sancta of the hearth, and otherwise
Become the angels of our buried dreams.
"What are we doing right?" unfeigned surprise,
Becoming bolder, asks, and thereby means
To warn us that a house of fleece and wool
Is necessarily ephemeral.

Evidence of Being Human

Not things that need be saved, as no one knows
Better than I, who ponder their disposal
Time after time, but having dared propose,
I put off implementing the proposal
On some weak pretext, saving year to year
Increasingly irrelevant odd clutter:
An unaccepted invitation, here
A scrawled receipt, in scarlet ink a letter

From someone whose first name I recognize
No longer (though I might if I worked at it)—
Yet even that I keep, a stolen prize
Rescued as it were from a fleeing pirate
To say: here was a man, was loved and hated,
To whom men came to talk and laugh or cry.
I keep it that it someday may be stated.
But when and where, to whom and how and why?

Dutiful

"Make Mother proud of you—and Father too."
Those good-boy chestnuts that I swallowed whole
Upset my stomach; still I played the role
Expected of me, doubting that they knew
How long I worked to make their dreams come true,
How hard I drove myself to reach each goal
That they might claim the prize, how great the toll
Those doubts I tried to, but could not, subdue
Demanded. They died proud of me, I guess.
(One hopes and wonders even at the end.)
Now that I've no one to make proud, I must
Invent their ghosts to proffer each success,
Unsure that they are pleased and queasy lest
They put their smiles on only to pretend.

Settled

Montreal: Aunt Mary, you've come home—
In ashes, true, but still to sit atop
Mount Royal, in marble splendor. You would come
Tobogganing upon the eastern slope
When you were in your teens, or so you said.
(With you one never knew where poetry
And truth divided.) Now that you are dead,
You have your years, not quite a century,
And nothing to your name, besides, and yet
Rooming in such a posh necropolis
May be the best coup you pulled off. The debt
I did not owe you has been paid; be this
A gift of beauty to one who believed
In beauty above all and was deceived.

Recalling What Would Have Been Aunt Mary's Ninety-Sixth Birthday

A letter comes from your old nursing home
Requesting (what else?) a donation to
Honor your birthday. Hardly something new;
My "mail" these days would add up to a tome
Of beggary in no time if I let it,
But this comes first-class mail and so at least
Is opened and perused before it meets
The trash. I really do not feel indebted
To hands so distant now in years and miles
That someone paid to care, and yet a pang
Of pain comes with the page—the lonely trials
You suffered when your bird no longer sang,
The old TV, for years your only friend,
Almost suffice to make fresh tears descend.

The Clock-Watcher

Even when listening to fugues of Bach,
Even while visiting my mother in
Her last few days, I had to have a clock
Or watch nearby. So it has always been.
Since first I learned to read the hands, I felt
Compelled to read them, maybe most compelled
When faced with nothing threatening to melt
Or burn, when time was only grace withheld.

Call it a habit; call it an obsession.
Is anyone so wise he understands
What drives the want with such absurd aggression
It cannot be held back, what makes their hands
So vital I would almost trade my own
Before I let their movement go unknown?

The Nonagenarian's Daughter's Complaint

What shall I tell her that will comfort her
Who, mourning death-in-life, has reached an age
When she has no contemporaries? Were
It possible to say *Time will assuage*
Your suffering—and soon and not sound crass,
Then I would find a way to say it, but
The words stop in my throat; I choke, alas,
On words I dare not utter lest they cut
Her wounds more deeply still. What shall I say
Beyond the platitudes we both despise?
Already cursed with too much life, she may
Go on to win the centenary prize
For staying on her train long past her station,
A passenger with no clear destination.

Mnemonics

Last night I rummaged through a squeaky drawer
I had not opened since I don't know when,
Searching I cannot recall what for
But finding nothing till I looked again

And in a corner saw a box of keys
Which I spilled out and put back one by one.
Forgotten, as it were, for centuries,
They seemed to open nothing I now own.

I first reacted with a vague delight
That in a life too neat and too uncovered
Some rooms and boxes still were recondite;
But now with their existence rediscovered,

I wish I could recall what they secured—
Those blackish keys that call to mind no more
Than that, whenever rust and thieves conspired,
I kept the key and threw away the door.

Did You

Did you remember to turn off the lights
And lock the door? You know you can't turn back;
You've come too far, and yet the imp that plays
On all your fears demands, "What if, what if?"
You try to wring each detail from your brain,
Recall each move before you left the house,
But all you call up are uncertainty
And, finally, a double memory
Whose halves are inconsistent: One says, yes,
You turned the key; the other, no, you closed
The door and walked. *Try not to think about
It* may be sound advice, but, as a mantra,
It fully fails: you worry all the more
Till it has made a shambles of a time.

Mother-in-Law

The well-bred coffee urn we got from her
Reminds me to make tea; her key unlocks
The red-and-yellow Chinese canister
And makes me think of our deposit box.
Tomorrow we sign papers to release
The funds sequestered by the iron court;
The wealth that bought her privilege and peace
Brought us to war, to litigate and part.
No act is so routine or commonplace
That it will fail to conjure up your face.

She let you wed an unregenerate Jew;
She said, "My dear, if that is what you seek . . ."
Saint Paul, the crafty Israelite who knew
The problems of uniting Jew and Greek,
Despaired of a deliverance through works
Advising circumcision of the heart.
Drayton countered, almost with a smirk,
"Since there's no help, come let us kiss and part."
But in the very breath of his attack
Declared the terms on which he would come back.

Where others would have plotted us apart
Or failing in such effort, held aloof,
She hid from the misgivings of her heart
In sacrificial gifts that seemed disproof
Of all my parents' talk of Gentile hate.

(I told them that the hatred was their own.)
Prating the foolish wisdom men will prate
To stave off madness yet not turn to stone,
I tell our friends our home would have endured
Our own despites had hers been less obscured.

Is this divorce the legacy she planned?
The dark proverbial vengeance of the dead?
I half believe it now and understand
How friends that I have criticized were led
By pity for themselves to freakish thoughts.
Or maybe we could not in any life,
Given our penchants to let wars be fought
On sacred ground, survive as man and wife.
I sip hot tea; her urn reflects my face
Distorted into anarchies of space.

Mockingbird Call

Whatifwhatifwhatif the creaking bird
That has adopted me cries night to night;
I wish he'd fly where he cannot be heard;
His raucous call has turned into a blight
Upon my life. What brought him to my sill?
(What silly questions men in dudgeon pose!)
Why not a thrush, a dove, a whippoorwill,
Or even a crow? Why not a bird who knows
That nights were made for sleep and calls for mates?
Whatifwhatif, and all that may go wrong
Pecks at my weary mind and aggravates
Its desolation with that mournful song
That melds into my sleep and haunts my dreams
And causes me to wake too soon, in screams.

De Senectute

Sunday, Sunday, my old friend,
Now that I'm old, you come
Too often to be privileged,
Too lacking in aplomb
To be received with flourishes
Or made to feel at home.

Sunday, Sunday, my old friend,
When and where this rift?
I don't remember quarreling;
I don't know why we drift
Together into separateness
Like giver and like gift.

Reproof

How often in my dreams I am expected
To try a case, entirely unprepared,
Or give a speech in Greek, so long neglected
I scarce recall the alphabet. Absurd
What those ascending through the ivory gates
Demand of me asleep, and stranger still
How terrified I am of what awaits
If I should prove unable to fulfill
The sheer impossible. Who are they? Who
That judge whose hands are always forming fists,
That steely voiced professor dressed in blue—
Authorities unable to resist
A chance to bully? Why do they not know
That I became one of them long ago?

On Noticing a Reception for the Class of 1966 at the Harvard Club

By thinking they look old,
I date myself the more;
I taught them just enrolled
As freshmen, long before

The Fall of Man or, should
I say, before I knew
Of it? What likelihood
This hall contains some who

Had me for Gen. Ed. A?
I would not recognize
Them or they, me today.
Youth is a grand disguise,

Which lasts until it fades;
They are all old, and I
Much older. Renegades
From life before the sky

Began to fall, we—they
And I—have merged into
The faceless old and gray,
Who face into the new,

Knowing it is not ours.
What more is there to say,
Except that time devours
And life is a cliché?

At Fifty-Nine

for Liz Cabot

It is not easy, but sometimes I can
Imagine being ten or twenty-two
Or forty-something, but a younger man
Again. It is not easy to undo
A decade or half-century of living
To get in touch with one who bears my name
And not much else that still is mine, but giving
The task some alcohol and candle flame,
Yes, I have managed it. But what you ask,
To see myself at seventy or older,
Is wholly too redoubtable a task
For my imagination, which, though bolder
Than many, is not bold enough to be
The bearer of its own mortality.

Another Birthday Poem for Myself— at Seventy-Two

Age is just a number—that is true.
But adages be damned—the numbers matter—
The scale that tells you straight-out how much fatter
You have become, the zeroes leading to
The decimal points in your accounts, the host
Of numbers adding up to how you score
On blood pressure, cholesterol, and more
Foretell both fate and fortune. Uppermost
Is: how much longer, where do numbers stop
Cold? Though no one boasts the magic gauge,
Truth is subtraction; as the gardeners lop
Off branch on branch to keep the tree alive,
The birthday message is *survive, survive.*

A Tour of the Interior

This is the train I never took;
This is my first unwritten book;
This is the sweetheart I never kissed;
These keys I lost but never missed.

This is the apple I never tasted;
This is the scrapbook I never pasted;
This is the poem I never wrote
(Whose lines professors never quote).

This is the coin I never tossed;
This is the river I never crossed;
These are the stairs I never climbed;
These are the rhymes I never rhymed.

This is the living I worked to make;
That is the train I meant to take.

For Mr. First

The first into the ocean
Or pool, prince of the beach,
While we put on our lotion,
You swam beyond our reach.

The first one to get drunk,
The first one to get laid,
You were the high school hunk
We envied. When you made

Your folks buy you a car
While we still learned to drive,
You seemed to us by far
The luckiest kid alive.

The first into TM
And first to call it bunk,
You joined AA but then
Felt better as a drunk.

Now first to meet the dragon
Who will devour us all,
You were, we hope, as arrogant
With him and walked as tall

The night he came to get you
As ever you had been
When starry-eyed, we let you
Steer us into sin.

Aunt and Uncle

She hated him but hid her hate
in hoverings more worthy of
a mother (maybe) than a mate.
But, then, there was not much to love

about him. As they wed, his aunt
summed him up neatly as "unfit
for bed or table," but one can't
be choosy when one's desperate—

and that she was. Her widowed mother
rationed kindness, also food,
and daily did her best to smother
a child who showed some aptitude

for anything except attending
to her. He was well-to-do
at least by her lights. Unascending
the thing he urinated through—

back then there was no treatment known
for this condition—still, he married;
he spoke in a soft monotone
remarks that, if his voice had carried,

would have embarrassed everyone
but him. And he was miserly.
Her years rolled by much as the sun
rolls by each day, eternity

compressed into a lifetime. What
had once seemed tolerable made
her bitter, narcissistic, but—
her grievances rehearsed—afraid

to do more than to scold him for
skipping a pill or taking no
umbrella in a drizzle or
not lowering the radio

at nine, the hour she retired,
while he stayed up to hear the news.
They shared a bed; no one inquired
what made this so-called couple choose

such lives as theirs. One day he moaned
that he felt sick, the next day, sicker;
when he said "hospital," she phoned
the cab stand; all they did was bicker

the whole way there. That night she got
a call that he was dying and
put on her clothes though she did not
phone for a cab until one hand

was gloved and coat and hat were on,
and when it came, the speed was spared,
and when she got there, he was gone,
and when they asked her if she cared

to see him, she said "no" and left.
And thirty years she played the part
of widow hopelessly bereft,
with a full purse and empty heart.

Rain Days

It's pouring out. The metaphor proves true
Too many ways. The water overflowing
The bird baths, channeling the avenue
Into a creek, reflects the ever-growing
Resentments long repressed but now cascading
In snide retorts. A statue seems to piss
In public with impunity, degrading
A street once stately. *It has come to this*,
They stage-whisper. I try retreating toward
The inner self I keep locked up and hidden
For trying times, but, once there, find a sword
Itching for use, and ghosts appear, unbidden,
Tapping the roof, demanding that the war
Continue till there's nothing left to pour.

Old Chairs

for Luann Landon

Miss Amy was a fixture in her house
And in the neighborhood a byword for
The woes that could befall a timid mouse
Long guarded by a cat. (Familiar lore
Has ways of multiplying out of hand;
Embroidered year to year, the dark tales told
Of youthful passion thwarted by the stand
Her father took against a handsome, bold,
But poor young man may have left truth behind;
She may have wanted too much, being young.)

When I knew her, she long had been defined
By sitting in her sewing room among
Old chairs. And when she spoke, one thought one heard
Another person's voice behind each word.

Unchanged

Two years before you died, you left this flat
For good, as you denied but must have known,
Humoring me, who in the nursing home
On Sunday visits all but told you that

Death itself was temporary. Still
You paid the rent each month and had the place
Cleaned on alternate Wednesdays and the lace
Curtains laundered twice each year until

Your last slow Wednesday. Was this so that I,
Returning here as your executor,
Would think of you as you had been before
Your body and your mind began to die?

If so, you almost managed; duty done,
I lock your rummaged desk. The sickly smells
Of two years spent in semi-private hells
Recede; your death becomes as new as one

That just occurred should be. But now my eye,
Caught by the calendar a yellow tack
Holds up, is troubled by a sudden lack
Of memory or reason. Though I try,

I can't remember which day of the week
It is, or fix the date today, until
I see your calendar is waiting still
With unturned pages, for your coming back.

On Reading of a Proposal to Blow Up the Moon

What further use to earth this satellite
When electricity can make the night
Brighter than seven moons at perigee
And do so without harrowing the sea
To flood the land or making ships abide
The rising and the ebbing of the tide
Or pushing lunatics to act the part
Of werewolves once a month? Who needs the art
The moon inspires? Just plug in a screen
And all that's worthy to be heard and seen
Appears. The awe the rising orange disc
Brings to one's soul, it brings at too much risk;
For those who care, computer programs can
Date Easter, Rosh Hashanah, Ramadan.

A Reproach to the Reproacher

Do not waste time, but use it up instead;
Then ask for more—oops, sorry, you are dead.

Reminders

I must remind
Myself to wind
The clock or it
Will soon omit
Reminding me
I have to be
Some place that I'd
As soon be tied
As go there though
Once told I go

Solutions

Too much paper piled up here?
Just pick it up and put it there.
Aha, your cluttered desk is clear.
Once it is there, you will not care,
Or when it bothers you, why, then
You'll bring the piles back here again.

Forgetful

My hair is falling out.
My stocks are going down.
I am consumed by doubt.
I often play the clown
without intending to.
My recall's growing short.

What did I say I'd do
but as a last resort ?

Lord Byron Lectures Us about Sex

The mottoes of the Georgian drinking clubs
Varied but little. Common was *May Prick
Nor Purse Ne'er Fail.* The looming Zeitgeist dubs
Its knights. I was a peer whose purse was sick;
The politics of dispossession rubs
Out many a predilection, and we pick
Our clubs to match our cups. Had mine been full,
Would I have turned out quite so liberal?

You never know with an aristocrat.
But, ah, my prick did not depend on coal
Mines leased below real value: when it sat,
It was imposing; when it rose, it stole
The accolades. (I boast—enough of that
For now.) Recall I lived when sex and soul
Were thought united and men, fat and bald,
Hopped bed to bed and no one was appalled.

So why not I? But, here, I must explain.
Although I did not deem myself "a gay"
(To use your language)—females I had lain
With did not think so either—I was, say,
Attracted and attractive to a skein
Of likely lads, some famous in their day.
As if belonging to an ancient Greek,
My prick chose which companions it should seek.

I chastised Bentham for attacking lust
That I considered natural, and when
He proffered an apology, I cussed
Him for its tepidness. Beware the pen
Aristocrats deploy. The violent thrust
Of prick and pen's the same for many men,
Relieving anger welled up in the heart
At what cannot be changed by craft or art.

At thirty-six I died an adolescent,
An adolescent painfully aware
Of being half a child, my evanescent
Visions of Greece's freedom in despair.
My frolics started early; incandescent,
They still outshine me. And they should. I swear.
Could I return as flesh, I would not yield
One dram of pleasure that my prick revealed.

A Soliloquy for Gabriel

*This poem is set at Aunt Julia's funeral, which takes place a
month after the closing scene of James Joyce's "The Dead."*

Fury is dead; my aged aunt is too,
But she outlived him by as many years
As he was old at death.

                One barely hears
The organ for the talking in the church:
Aunt Julia's friends—yes, everyone who knew
Her, meaning half of Dublin—fill each pew
With bodies and with noise. Though one might search
Old world and new, no people would he find
Religious as the Irish; yet in church
Before the priest walks down the aisle, they mind
No manners but their own.

                   It's Bach, I think.
A Lutheran, but if there are no words,
There is no heresy, and none need shrink
From listening to notes. Oh, it's absurd,
All right, to think about what can't be heard
Or read here if it smacks of heresy.

Requiem aeternam dona eis;

Aunt Julia, though, was never one to rest
Or, for that matter, mortify the flesh.
The priest who urges us to is obese;
I'll bet he mortifies the flesh. He blessed
Her body—didn't he? I can't refresh
My recollection. But he must have. What
If he did not? O Jesus, nothing but
A day of worry here.

Libera me
De morte aeterna. I am not sure
I want to be delivered on that day
The trumpet blasts, the saved rise up, they say,
To sing with angels. Are the harps they play
As sweet as ours? And are their tones as pure
And rich as Bach's?

           Shall I receive the host?
I shall. I must. Lest disrespect or worse
Be thought afoot. Oh, dear Aunt Julia, whom
I truly loved—I could not let her hearse
Go to the grave with gossip.

           Ah, the toast
I gave at her last Christmas party such
A little time ago, and now so much
Is changed, all over, of all things, galoshes.
She loved him more; I did not need to know.
Fury is dead. What makes a woman think
She is worth dying for?

When did he bless
Aunt Julia's body?

Some men die for drinks
And some for love. Myself, when there is snow,
I wear galoshes. *Agnus Dei, qui*
Tollis, tollis peccata mundi,
Have mercy on Aunt Julia, Fury, me.

Amos

One thing for sure: he could attract attention
Telling them how their crisscrossed enemies
Would pay for sins too numerous to mention
Save by example. Even now one sees
The swelling crowd delighting to hear judgment
Pronounced on nations far too deaf to hear,
Perceiving a supposed acknowledgment
That they were, if not sinless, fairly near.

Then, wham, he turned the logic of his fury
Upon them, and they had no place to hide;
The God who was impartial judge and jury
Would treat them as He did their neighbors. Tried
And found as guilty, they, whom He had known
Among all nations best, He would disown.

Ezekiel

He is most graphic in his images
(And almost pornographic in a few);
No wonder that an old tradition says
He barely passed the canon and was too
Explicit for the underaged. But here
Is ruthless poetry, the essence of
The Hebrew scriptures, language that could sear
An angel's wing. His wife, his dearest love,
Was taken from him overnight, and he,
Forbidden by the Lord to mourn her, let
Loose wrath as palpable as any we
Shall ever meet. He spewed out God's hate; yet
In part because of him, some bleached bones rose
And put on flesh as though it had been clothes.

The Prisoner

Rejoice in the Lord alway: and *again I say, Rejoice.*
Philippians 4:4, King James Bible

He seldom is sought out amid the rats;
Yet humbled to the point of arrogance
And never one to wait upon events,
He issues claims of victory, knowing that

His time is short, his enterprise undone.
Less cunning than his master and less full
Of charity, but less parochial,
This epileptic with his sight half-gone

Called some his brothers who are now ashamed
To visit him—or do they think him mad?
The running rumor is that things look bad;
There is unrest and someone must be blamed.

Though once he wrote a poem about love,
He is not lovable except by choice.
Now, when he importunes them to rejoice,
What in creation is he thinking of?

Galatians

Of all Paul's letters, this is most severe,
Most personal, most likely to have been
Preserved intact. His wrath we almost hear
Rather than read. We feel his prickly skin
Beneath his words, defending himself from
Accusing tongues denying he had leave
To tell the Gentiles that they could become
Among the chosen if they would believe
What he believed. We cannot even guess
What had been said once between him and James
Or if his fray with Peter came to less
Or more than he let on; we know he blames
Rank heretics for contradictions, then
Claims his apostleship from God, not men.

Would He Say This?

I dreamed—or daydreamed, I'm no longer sure—
I stepped into a heaven peopled by
Jews, only Jews, almost a caricature
On Jewishness, hooked noses, beards, if I
Am not mistaken, two men haggling
Over a price or point of law. My first
Thought was: *Misunderstanding—not a thing*
About this place is heavenly, and worst
Of all, I don't belong. But then I grew
Much more inquisitive. *Was Einstein there?*
I did not ask, for suddenly I knew
That Jesus was the one I most would care
To speak to, but his voice fell harsh and cold,
"My people suffered for the lies you told."

Male, Female, and the Church Fathers

Born not of women but (as they supposed)
Of earth and water, bearded saints whose eyes
Could pierce whatever had been clothed or closed
Denounced the female as a thin disguise
For levity, if not concupiscence,
Demanded that her head be covered and
Her voice, at least in Church establishments,
Be hushed. One wonders: did they understand
At all, or understand too well, that in
The Gospels (widely different pen to pen),
Women in mourning first learn Christ has been
Raised from the tomb and rush to tell the men,
Who must be shown before they will believe
The news the women gratefully receive.

No Doubt?

A healthy skepticism is, no doubt
(See how a pun can lead to paradox),
An asset in a world of claims. Without
It, one's a goose and prey to every fox
The woods can hold. To not end up their feast,
One has to question motives, every claim
Assessed against those motives, every beast
Presumed a fox known by whatever name.

But shouldn't one be skeptical also
Of skepticism? After questioning
Beyond endurance, what do skeptics know?
Credulity may be the very thing
That saves those who without it would succumb
To mind-made beasts there's no escaping from.

The Plagiarists

Theoretically, of course, a first
Exists for everything, but where
Trails peter out and there

Is only arrant darkness, to ensnare
The primal thought is labor cursed
By light denied. Though versed

In manuscripts that have survived the rage
Of mobs and armies, the neglect
Of scholars, we suspect

That every monument of intellect
Was sketched on someone else's page
And copied by some "sage."

Nothing new under the sun was said
By someone wise, anonymous, and dead.

Bach

Deserving a cathedral or at least
A gilded hall affecting High Baroque,
Bach's weighty organ works are finely pieced
Upon a spool that weighs an ounce at most
To be replayed in, say, a car, and so
As I ride on expressways and along
The city's sprawl, blared from my stereo,
The fugue in D is mingled with the song
Of windshield wipers, engine fans, and tires.
Could he be at my side, what would he say?
"It's taste that counts; do what the age requires,"
Or "How could you have gall enough to play
Music meant to swell the contrite heart
In this swift arrogance devoid of art?"

On Book II, Satire V, of Horace

for Mike Juster

Only a genius of a poet would
Dare to attempt, much less to realize,
A poem on Ulysses wanting good
Advice on how he could regain the size
Fortune he'd had before he went to war
And tarried for adventure. Others might
Have shown the onetime warrior a bore
Whose talk was crops and herds, his lips sealed tight
About what he had heard and seen and done,
Or prone to dwell on every escapade
Till he seemed self-suffused. But only one
Possessed that bitter-comic gift which made
His hero get advice to offer shares
Of charm and cheek to childless millionaires.

To a Certain Poet

Apollo and Erato stay away?
Well, little wonder, given Eris's
Propensity to visit every day.
A poet must, like others, winnow his
Guest list if he expects the class-A crowd
To show up on demand. (Kings only mix
Uneasily with commoners; the loud
Contentious fool is shunned by fools who fix
A silent gaze.) Some argument is spice
To pallid food? No doubt. But even on
Olympus, Zeus will gladly sacrifice
That spice for godly calm. With Eris gone,
Who knows what peace will prove? Perhaps no more
Than you and tedium in strange rapport.

Comprehension Test

No poet who has ever penned
A verse that none could comprehend
Has ever thought the fault might be
His own lack of lucidity.

The Poet's Drug

The act of writing could itself contract
Whatever swirled around him into one
Dim, distant moon to be ignored until
The paper had been filled, the poem done.
And while he wrote, there was no good or ill,
His body had no weight, his mind was stoked
By stuff as strong as that shot up or smoked.

Travelogue

Past Lovers Lake the road veers sharply south:
You see some barns, deserted, nondescript;
Far on your right the river forms a crypt,
Then forks in semblance of a viper's mouth.

The natives say this fork the river makes
Portends the course it later will pursue,
That past its falls the mainstream slithers to
A brackish pool that swarms with torpid snakes.

There is an ancient map that shows this road
Winding south and west to some great city
At which the river meets the SEA OF PITY.
(All other names paled out or never showed.)

The natives know of no such place as this;
None hereabouts have even heard of it.
They say the road just narrows bit by bit
And ends abruptly at a precipice.

Who Told You?

Who told you life was one straight line
Or shining arc or perfect square?
You turn and turn at every sign
That you'll find something worthy there

If you just take this turn or that.
(Illusion laughs both last and loud.)
You watch for tree limbs, bending at
Mere shadows, too; you end up bowed

And bloody from the ones you miss.
Who told you that one day you'd reach,
By walking far, a place of bliss?
No limit to the lies they teach

The young, eh? Or is this a thing
Wholly of your imagining?

The Cave Dweller

I once could not imagine turning out
The light, not having heard news at eleven,
But now that I am old, I do without
It, positing that if I wake in heaven,
Someone may whisper it, and if on earth,
The news will be there by the morning light.
No need till then to rediscern the dearth
Of kindliness, the plethora of blight.

This is a way of saying, I suppose,
The world gets on without me very well;
That it took years for me to learn this shows
How one not overly naive can dwell
In shocking ignorance of who he is
And how much of the world is really his.

For Hobo

Obit *25 February 2006*

The vet said it was cruel to force more life
On you in kidney failure. We agreed.
You had lived twenty years—your first in strife
That feral cats endure, the rest in need
Of nothing. Friends of ours would often note
How fortunate you were, but we would smile;
Your quick kiss, your soft purr, your silken coat
Enriched us beyond words. And you had style
And showed it when you leapt on laps or ate
In dainty mouthfuls. Skein of mottled gray
And white, you deserved better than to wait
In pain for death to come to you the way
It was approaching, but you will be missed
Each night, not with us to be stroked and kissed.

Cat Ghost

A gust of wind made that swift-moving shadow
Traverse the floor beside the window.

Only three seconds, and I saw it for
Just what it was and nothing more.

But for those seconds, my beloved Hobo,
Gone a week, you were that shadow

Approaching breakfast on your silent feet,
Wondering what there was to eat.

I did not rise to fetch food from your cupboard;
I did no more than feel an inward

Disappointment or, say, vacancy
Destined to stay part of me.

To Summer Fading

Others may miss you; I shall not.
Happiness and being hot
Are my antipodes; let fall
Assert dominion over all
The Northern Hemisphere, I say.

Yet something longs for one more day
Of brooding over discontents
With rich ripe fruit and indolence.

Rural Christmas

Christmas Eve—the FM stereo
Delivers tasteful music and discreet
Commercials; this palatial inn has no
Space like a manger, just good things to eat,
Fine wine to drink, a comfortable bed.
The animals asleep upon the hay
Will never wake, unless, dispirited,
They wander into human dreams to play.

The year of rage recedes into the night,
Which holds no special star to guide the wise
To Bethlehem, itself a tourist site
And little else. God is beyond surmise,
And man-made comforts must suffice to fill
One's emptiness, one's indolence of will.

A New Year's Poem

It's time to usher out the holiday,
Harvest the ornaments, take down the tree,
And put assorted Christmas lights away
Until next year. But when you get to be
Above a certain age, a whisper wants
To know how many next years still remain,
And if you slack your work, that whisper haunts
The ultimate recesses of your brain.

It's time that winter be allowed to act
Her age and be herself without the masks
December forced on her; that month is packed
In neatly lettered boxes. New Year's asks
No new resolve, only acceptance of
Diminished warmth and unrecited love.

Early January

Isn't this the day I prayed for?
Isn't snow a welcome sight?
Nothing moves; the day was made for
Setting promises aright.

Write the letters; read the presents
(Books that Santa's reindeer dropped);
Bake that bread much loved by peasants.
Act for once as though time stopped.

Maybe no one will reset it;
Why must every gift be brief?
Phone is ringing—shall I get it?—
Later feigning disbelief,

After roads are fit for travel
And no promises are kept,
That intentions could unravel,
That I might as well have slept.

Grace

As one who, reading late into the night,
When overcome by sleep, turns off the light
And yields whatever he can sense by sight

To what the gates of ivory or of horn
Will send him, sightless as a child unborn,
To goad, amuse, remind, reveal, or warn,

So may I turn a light off and embrace
With resignation, better still with grace,
The dreamless sleep that all awake must face.

And the Others

Some find The Light in literature,
Others in fine art,
And some persist in being sure
The Light shines in the heart.

Some find The Light in alcohol;
Some, in the sexual spark;
Some never find The Light at all
And make do with the dark,

And one might guess that these would be
A gloomy lot indeed,
But, no, The Light they never see
They think they do not need.

The Effect of Hearing the Sublime

Odysseus, who heard the sirens sing,
was not enraptured by another thing
he heard from human lips; fools muttering
and golden sounds that proved the flutist's skill,
which other men said gave their hearts a thrill,
to him were equally dislikable.
He knew that he would never hear again
the sounds he would have died for had his men
been able to hear what he said to them,
which was, "Steer toward the music, though it means
we shall not land upon familiar scenes
nor want to, once this music intervenes."

Oh Where

Where did you go, my dear, my day;
Where, oh where, did you go?
To market, to maker of market: to say
Too much of the little I know.

Where did you go, my dear, my year;
Why did you flee from me?
I went from here to there to here
Loitering breathlessly.

Where did you go, my life, my own,
Decades gone in a wink?
Some things are better left unknown,
Some thoughts too thick to think.

DAVID BERMAN
(1934–2017) was born
on September 11, 1934,
in New York City and
raised in Hollywood,
Florida. Licensed as
an attorney in 1963,
Berman clerked for
Justice Jacob Spiegel
of the Massachusetts
Supreme Judicial Court,
and from 1964 to 1967
served as Assistant
Attorney General of
Massachusetts under

Edward Brooke. From 1967 until his death, he had a private practice
in the Boston area with an emphasis on business litigation.

Berman also had a parallel career as a poet. While working in Boston
in the late 1950s, he took Robert Lowell's poetry seminar at Boston
University. As a law student at Harvard, he was permitted to take
Archibald MacLeish's poetry course, which he called the "high point"
of his week, and where he met and befriended the poet Bruce Bennett.
While at Harvard, he was frequently published in the *Harvard Advocate*.
Over the years, Berman published a number of poems in literary journals
such as the *Formalist*, *Piedmont Literary Review*, *Sparrow*, *Orbis*, *Iambs
and Trochees*, and *Pivot*. He also published three chapbooks: *Future
Imperfect* (State Street Press, 1982), *Slippage* (Robert L. Barth, 1996),
and *David Berman: Greatest Hits 1965–2002* (Pudding House, 2002).

Berman was a longtime member of the Powow River Poets of
Newbury, Massachusetts. In addition, he was a member of the Harvard
Club, a trustee of the Cantata Singers, and Vice Échanson and Vice
Conseiller Gastronomique Honoraire of the Boston chapter of La
Confrérie de la Chaîne des Rôtisseurs. He passed away on June 22,
2017, after battling cancer for several months.

ALSO FROM ABLE MUSE PRESS

Jacob M. Appel, *The Cynic in Extremis: Poems*

William Baer, *Times Square and Other Stories; New Jersey Noir: A Novel;*
New Jersey Noir (Cape May): A Novel;
New Jersey Noir (Barnegat Light):A Novel

Lee Harlin Bahan, *A Year of Mourning (Petrarch): Translation*

Melissa Balmain, *Walking in on People (Able Muse Book Award for Poetry)*

Ben Berman, *Strange Borderlands: Poems; Figuring in the Figure: Poems*

David Berman, *Progressions of the Mind: Poems*

Lorna Knowles Blake, *Green Hill (Able Muse Book Award for Poetry)*

Michael Cantor, *Life in the Second Circle: Poems*

Catherine Chandler, *Lines of Flight: Poems*

William Conelly, *Uncontested Grounds: Poems*

Maryann Corbett, *Credo for the Checkout Line in Winter: Poems;*
Street View: Poems; In Code: Poems

Will Cordeiro, *Trap Street (Able Muse Book Award for Poetry)*

Brian Culhane, *Remembering Lethe: Poems*

John Philip Drury, *Sea Level Rising: Poems*

Rhina P. Espaillat, *And After All: Poems*

Anna M. Evans, *Under Dark Waters: Surviving the* Titanic: *Poems*

Stephen Gibson, *Frida Kahlo in Fort Lauderdale: Poems*

D. R. Goodman, *Greed: A Confession: Poems*

Carrie Green, *Studies of Familiar Birds: Poems*

Margaret Ann Griffiths, *Grasshopper: The Poetry of M A Griffiths*

Janis Harrington, *How to Cut a Woman in Half: Poems*

Katie Hartsock, *Bed of Impatiens: Poems*

Elise Hempel, *Second Rain: Poems*

Jan D. Hodge, *Taking Shape: Carmina figurata;*
The Bard & Scheherazade Keep Company: Poems

Ellen Kaufman, *House Music: Poems; Double-Parked, with Tosca: Poems*

Len Krisak, *Say What You Will (Able Muse Book Award for Poetry)*

Emily Leithauser, *The Borrowed World (Able Muse Book Award for Poetry)*

Hailey Leithauser, *Saint Worm: Poems*

Carol Light, *Heaven from Steam: Poems*

Kate Light, *Character Shoes: Poems*

April Lindner, *This Bed Our Bodies Shaped: Poems*

Martin McGovern, *Bad Fame: Poems*

Jeredith Merrin, *Cup: Poems*

Richard Moore, *Selected Poems;*
The Rule That Liberates: An Expanded Edition: Selected Essays

Richard Newman, *All the Wasted Beauty of the World: Poems*

Alfred Nicol, *Animal Psalms: Poems*

Deirdre O'Connor, *The Cupped Field (Able Muse Book Award for Poetry)*

Frank Osen, *Virtue, Big as Sin (Able Muse Book Award for Poetry)*

Alexander Pepple (Editor), *Able Muse Anthology;*
Able Muse: A Review of Poetry, Prose & Art (semiannual, winter 2010 on)

James Pollock, *Sailing to Babylon: Poems*

Aaron Poochigian, *The Cosmic Purr: Poems; Manhattanite*
(Able Muse Book Award for Poetry)

Tatiana Forero Puerta, *Cleaning the Ghost Room: Poems*

Jennifer Reeser, *Indigenous: Poems; Strong Feather: Poems*

John Ridland, *Sir Gawain and the Green Knight (Anonymous): Translation;*
Pearl (Anonymous): Translation

Stephen Scaer, *Pumpkin Chucking: Poems*

Hollis Seamon, *Corporeality: Stories*

Ed Shacklee, *The Blind Loon: A Bestiary*

Carrie Shipers, *Cause for Concern (Able Muse Book Award for Poetry)*

Matthew Buckley Smith, *Dirge for an Imaginary World*
(Able Muse Book Award for Poetry)

Susan de Sola, *Frozen Charlotte: Poems*

Barbara Ellen Sorensen, *Compositions of the Dead Playing Flutes: Poems*

Rebecca Starks, *Time Is Always Now: Poems; Fetch Muse: Poems*

Sally Thomas, *Motherland: Poems*

Paulette Demers Turco (Editor), *The Powow River Poets Anthology II*

Rosemerry Wahtola Trommer, *Naked for Tea: Poems*

Wendy Videlock, *Slingshots and Love Plums: Poems;*
The Dark Gnu and Other Poems; Nevertheless: Poems

Richard Wakefield, *A Vertical Mile: Poems; Terminal Park: Poems*

Gail White, *Asperity Street: Poems*

Chelsea Woodard, *Vellum: Poems*

Rob Wright, *Last Wishes: Poems*

www.ablemusepress.com

Made in the USA
Las Vegas, NV
30 January 2024

85095416R00059